CORONAVIRUS

AND

CHRIST

Other books by John Piper

The Dangerous Duty of Delight

Desiring God

Don't Waste Your Life

Fifty Reasons Why Jesus Came to Die

God Is the Gospel

A Hunger for God

Let the Nations Be Glad!

The Pleasures of God

Reading the Bible Supernaturally

Seeing and Savoring Jesus Christ

Spectacular Sins

A Sweet and Bitter Providence

What Jesus Demands from the World

When I Don't Desire God

Why I Love the Apostle Paul

CORONAVIRUS
AND
CHRIST

John Piper

:: **CROSSWAY**®

WHEATON, ILLINOIS

Trade paperback ISBN: 978-1-4335-7359-0
ePub ISBN: 978-1-4335-7362-0
PDF ISBN: 978-1-4335-7360-6
Mobipocket ISBN: 978-1-4335-7361-3

Library of Congress Control Number: 2020936307

Crossway is a publishing ministry of Good News Publishers.

LSC		28	27	26	25	24	23	22	21	20
14	13	12	11	10	9	8	7	6	5	4	3	2	1

CONTENTS

THE OCCASION:
CORONAVIRUS

I AM WRITING THIS little book in the last days of March 2020, on the front end of the global pandemic known as the coronavirus, or technically, "coronavirus disease 2019" (abbreviated COVID-19). The virus affects the lungs, and in the worst cases kills by suffocation.

The first death by the virus was reported in China on January 11, 2020. Today as I write, there are hundreds of thousands of cases of infection worldwide, with tens of thousands of deaths. There is no known cure—yet.

By the time you read this, you will know far better than I how things will develop. So I need not detail the measures being taken to slow the spread of the virus or the economic toll being exacted. Social mingling, travel, conferences, church gatherings, theaters, restaurants, sporting events, and businesses are nearing a standstill.

This is not unprecedented—either globally or in America. In the global influenza epidemic of 1918 (to use the estimates of the Centers for Disease Control), fifty million people around the world died.[1] Over five hundred thousand of those were in the United States. People felt symptoms in the morning and were dead by nightfall. Bodies were picked up from front porches to be carted away to graves dug by bulldozers. A man was shot for not wearing a mask. Schools were closed. Ministers spoke of Armageddon.

Of course precedents prove nothing. The past is warning, not fate. Nevertheless, this is a time when the fragile form of this world is felt. The seemingly solid foundations are shaking. The question we should be asking is, Do we have a Rock under our feet? A Rock that cannot be shaken—ever?

Part 1

THE GOD WHO REIGNS
OVER THE CORONAVIRUS

Chapter 1

COME TO THE ROCK

I AM MOVED TO WRITE because playing the odds is a fragile place to put your hope. Odds like 3 percent versus 10 percent, youth versus old age, compromised health versus no history of disease, rural versus urban, self-isolated versus home meeting with friends. Playing the odds provides little hope. It is not a firm place to stand.

There is a better way. There is a better place to stand: a Rock of certainty rather than the sand of probabilities.

WHEN CANCER CAME

I recall being told on December 21, 2005, that I had prostate cancer. For the next several weeks, all the talk was about odds. Odds with waiting to see. Odds with medications. Odds with homeopathic procedures. Odds with radical surgery. My wife, Noël, and I took these numbers seriously. But in the evening, we would smile at each other and think, *Our hope is not in the odds. Our hope is in God.*

We did *not* mean, "It is 100 percent certain God will heal me, while doctors can only give me odds." The Rock we are talking about is better than that. Yes, better than healing.

Even before the phone call from the doctor telling me I had cancer, God had already reminded me in a remarkable way about the Rock under my feet. After my usual annual exam, the urologist had looked at me and said, "I'd like to do a biopsy."

Really? I thought. "When?"

"Right now, if you have the time."

"I'll make time."

While he was going to get the machine, and while I was changing into the typical unflattering blue gown, there was time for me to ponder what was happening. *So he thinks I may have cancer.* As my future in this world began to change before my eyes, God brought to my mind something I had read recently in the Bible.

GOD SPOKE

Now, let's be clear. I don't hear voices. At least I never have. My confidence that God speaks is rooted in the fact that the Bible is his word. (More on that in the next chapter.) He has spoken, once for all, and he still speaks in his word. The Bible, rightly understood, *is* the voice of God.

Here is what he said to me in that urologist's office as I waited for the biopsy that would confirm that I had cancer. "John Piper, this is not wrath. Live or die, you will be with me." That's my paraphrase. Here's what he actually said:

> God has not destined us for wrath, but to obtain salvation through our Lord Jesus Christ, who died for us so that whether we are awake or asleep we might live with him. (1 Thess. 5:9–10)

Awake or asleep—that is, live or die—I will be alive with God. How can that be? I am a sinner. I have never lived a day of my life—not *one*—without falling short of God's standards of love and holiness. So how can this be? How can God say, "You, John Piper, will be with me—live or die"?

God didn't even wait for the question before he answered. It's because of Jesus. Jesus alone. Because of his death, there will be no wrath toward me. Not because of my perfection. My sins, my guilt, and my punishment fell on my Savior, Jesus Christ. He "died for us." That's what his word says. Therefore, I am free from guilt. Free from punishment. Secure in God's merciful favor. "Live or die," God said, "you will be with me."

That is very different from playing the odds with cancer—or with the coronavirus. This is a firm Rock under my feet. It is not fragile. It is not sand. I would like it to be a Rock under your feet. That is why I am writing.

IS THE ROCK SOLID ONLY IN THE BY-AND-BY?

But that's not all. Someone might read that and say, "Religious people like you can find hope only in the by-and-by. If they are safe beyond the grave, they have what they want. But this 'voice of God' they talk about offers little involvement right now. God got everything started in creation, I suppose, and makes happily-ever-after endings. But what about in between? Where is he now—right now, during this coronavirus outbreak?"

Well, I guess I do put a really high value on joy in the presence of God after death for unending billions of years.

As opposed to, say, endless suffering. That seems reasonable to me. But the Rock under my feet (the one I would like you to share) really is under my feet *now*. Now!

The coronavirus pandemic is where I live. Where we all live. And if it weren't the coronavirus, it would be the cancer just waiting to recur. Or the unprovoked pulmonary embolism from 2014 just waiting to break off and go to my brain and turn me into a mindless man who will never write another sentence. Or a hundred other unforeseen calamities that could take me—and you—down at any moment.

The Rock I am talking about is under my feet now. I *could* say that the Rock is under my feet now just because hope beyond the grave is *present* hope. The *object* of hope is future. The *experience* of hope is present. And that present experience is powerful.

Hope is power. Present power. Hope keeps people from killing themselves—now. It helps people get out of bed and go to work—now. It gives meaning to daily life, even locked-down, quarantined, stay-at-home life—now. It liberates from the selfishness of fear and greed—now. It empowers love and risk taking and sacrifice—now.

So be careful before you belittle the by-and-by. It just may be that when your by-and-by is beautiful and sure, your here and now will be sweet and fruitful.

HIS FINGERS IN VIRUSES

That's what I *could* say in defense of God's sweet word to me in the urologist's office: "Live or die, you will be with me." Such hope (through the death and resurrection of Jesus) makes me want to pour out my life for the good of others *now*—especially their eternal good. It makes me passionate not to waste my life. It takes away dithering. It fills me with a zeal to make the greatness of Jesus Christ known. It makes me want to spend and be spent (2 Cor. 12:15) to bring as many people with me as I can into everlasting joy.

But even though that's what I *could* say, when someone objects that Piper's God specializes in the by-and-by, not the here and now, it's not the only thing that needs to be said.

In fact, what I'm about to say will probably make someone object, "Whoa! That's way too much involvement for God in the here and now. Now you've gone from a God who only fixes the future to a God with his fingers in viruses."

NOT "I'M FINE," BUT "I FEEL FINE"

Let's put it this way. People would often ask me before my cancer diagnosis, "How's your health?" And I would answer, "Fine." I don't answer that way anymore. I say, "I feel fine." There's a difference. The day before I went for that annual prostate exam, I *felt* fine. The day after, I was told I had cancer. In other words, I was *not* fine. So even as I write these words, I do not know if I am fine. I feel fine. Way better than I deserve. For all I know, I have cancer right now. Or perhaps a blood clot. Or the coronavirus.

What's the point? The point is this: the ultimate reason we ought not to say, "I *am* fine," is that God alone knows and decides if you are fine—now. To say, "I am fine," when you don't *know* if you are fine, and you don't *control* if you are fine, is like saying, "Tomorrow, I will go to Chicago and do business there," when you have no idea if you will even be alive tomorrow, let alone doing business in Chicago.

Here's what the Bible says about a sentence like that:

Come now, you who say, "Today or tomorrow we will go into such and such a town and spend a year there and trade and make a profit"—yet you do not know what tomorrow will bring. What is your life? For you are a mist that appears for a little time and then vanishes. Instead you ought to say, "If the Lord wills, we will live and do this or that." (James 4:13–15)

So the God who is involved only in the by-and-by just evaporated. That's the effect of the bright sunlight of biblical truth on the ephemeral mists of our opinions.

IF HE DECIDES, WE DO THIS OR THAT

The Rock I stand on (and want you to stand on) is the Rock of God's action in the world *now*, and *forever*. "If the Lord wills," the Bible says, "we will live." That's about as involved now as you can get. Not just, "Whether you live or die, you will be with God," but also, "God will decide if you live or die—now."

And not just live or die. He's even more involved than that. "If the Lord wills, we will . . . *do this or that*." Nothing is excluded from "this or that." He is totally involved. Totally. *This* health, or *that* sickness. *This* economic collapse, or *that* recovery. *This* breath, or not.

Which means that while I waited in the doctor's office for the biopsy machine to arrive, God could have said (which he did later), "Fear not. Whether you live or die, you will be with me. *And* in the meantime, while you live, nothing will happen to you—nothing!—that I do not appoint. If I decide, you will live. If I decide, you will die. And until you die at my decision, I will decide if you do this or that. Get to work."

This is my Rock—for today, tomorrow, and eternity.

COME TO THE ROCK

This book is my invitation for you to join me on the solid Rock, Jesus Christ. What that means will, I hope, become clear. My aim is to show why God in Christ is the Rock at this moment in history—in this pandemic of the coronavirus—and what it is like to stand on his mighty love.

Chapter 2

A SOLID FOUNDATION

IT MATTERS LITTLE WHAT I THINK about the coronavirus—or about anything else, for that matter. But it matters forever what God thinks. He is not silent about what he thinks. Scarcely a page in the Bible is irrelevant for this crisis.

SOLID AND SWEET

My voice is grass. God's voice is granite. "The grass withers, and the flower falls, but the word of the Lord remains forever" (1 Pet. 1:24–25). Jesus said that God's words in Scripture "cannot be broken" (John 10:35). What God says is "true, and righteous altogether" (Ps. 19:9). His word is, therefore, a firm foundation for life. "You have founded [your testimonies] forever" (Ps. 119:152). Listening to God, and believing him, is like building your house on a rock, not on sand (Matt. 7:24).

His word is the kind of counsel you want to heed. "He is wonderful in counsel and excellent in wisdom" (Isa. 28:29). "His understanding is beyond measure" (Ps. 147:5). When he gives counsel about the coronavirus, it is firm, unshakable, lasting. "The counsel of the LORD stands forever" (Ps. 33:11). "His way is perfect" (2 Sam. 22:31).

Therefore, his words are sweet and precious. "More to be desired are they than gold: . . . sweeter also than honey and drippings of the honeycomb" (Ps. 19:10). Indeed, they are the sweetness of everlasting life: "Lord, to whom shall we go? You have the words of eternal life" (John 6:68).

Therefore, in the best and worst of times, God's words bring unshakable peace and joy. Surely it must be so. My prayer is that all who read this book would share the experience of the prophet Jeremiah: "Your words became to me a joy and the delight of my heart" (Jer. 15:16).

And mark this: the sweetness of God's word is not lost in this historic moment of bitter providence—not if we have learned the secret of "sorrowful, yet always rejoicing" (2 Cor. 6:10). We will see more fully later what this secret is. But here it is now in a single sentence. The secret of "sorrowful, yet always rejoicing" is this: *knowing that the same sovereignty that could stop the coronavirus, yet doesn't, is the very sovereignty that sustains the soul in it.* Indeed, more than sustains—sweetens. Sweetens with hope that God's purposes are kind, even in death—for those who trust him.

HOW DO YOU KNOW?

All the more urgent, therefore, is the question, How do you know that the Bible is the word of God? My short answer is that there is a divine glory that shines through it, which fits perfectly with the God-shaped template in your heart—like sprocket and gear, hand and glove, fish and water, wings and air, the final piece of a jigsaw puzzle.

To which I can imagine someone saying, "That sounds sort of mystical and subjective. Why do you answer like that?"

Because fifty years ago, when I was struggling to know what I should build my life on, I realized that the scholarly, historical arguments for the Bible would not work for most of the world. Why? Because, while true and helpful to a point, they cannot be followed by an eight-year-old child, a newly encountered preliterate villager in a remote South Pacific jungle, or an ordinary person in the West with little formal education. And yet it seemed obvious to me that God intended for such people to hear the word of God and believe—without leaping into the dark.

BIBLICAL FAITH IS NOT A LEAP IN THE DARK

The biblical view of faith is not a leap in the dark. It is warranted and well-grounded. It's called *faith* not because it has no foundation. It's called *faith* because it involves trust. Jesus didn't call the *believers* blind; he called the *un*believers blind (Matt. 15:14). "Seeing they do not see" (Matt. 13:13). Saving faith in God's word is based on "seeing." Real seeing.

Seeing what? The Bible answers like this: Satan does all he can to blind "the minds of the unbelievers, to keep them from *seeing* the light of the gospel of the glory of Christ, who is the image of God" (2 Cor. 4:4).

In other words, there is a kind of spiritual light that shines through the gospel—the biblical story of salvation. What kind of light? It's the light "of the glory of Christ, who is the image of God." This is not magical. It's not mystical in the sense of something appearing that is really not there. Jesus Christ is the kind of divine-human person whose moral and spiritual and supernatural glory—his beauty and worth and greatness—shines through God's word. It authenticates Scripture as true.

GOD-SHAPED TEMPLATE IN YOUR SOUL

This is why I say there is a divine glory that shines through the Scriptures that fits perfectly with the God-shaped template in your heart. In that way, it authenticates the truth and value of the Bible.

Yes, I do believe that there is a God-shaped template—a kind of indirect knowledge of God—in every human soul. The Bible puts it like this. Speaking of all humanity, it says, "What can be known about God is plain to them. . . . Although they knew God, they did not honor him as God" (Rom. 1:19, 21).

The Bible teaches that this *knowing* in every soul makes us all responsible to see the glory of God in nature. In the same way, we are also responsible to see the glory of God in

Jesus through his word. "The heavens declare the glory of God" (Ps. 19:1). We are obliged to see it and give thanks. So also the Son of God displays the glory of God. And we are responsible to see it and worship. The apostle John says, "We have seen his glory, glory as of the only Son from the Father" (John 1:14).

This is the self-authenticating glory that shines from God's word and gives us a warranted, well-grounded foundation for believing that the Christian Scriptures are from God.

TECHNOLOGY VERSUS TASTE

The way we come to know the glory of God in Scripture is similar to the way we know that honey is honey. Science and technology may say that this jar contains honey because of chemical experiments—just like biblical scholars can argue compellingly that the Bible is historically reliable. But most people are not scientists or scholars. We know that this is honey because we taste it.

Similarly, there is a divine sweetness in the glory of God in the message of the Bible. It touches a part of us that we know was put there by God. "How sweet are your words to my taste, sweeter than honey to my mouth!" (Ps. 119:103). "Oh, taste and see that the LORD is good!" (Ps. 34:8). This is a real seeing and tasting. It is not make believe. It sees and tastes what is really there.

YES TO THE ROCK OF OUR COMFORT

So when Jesus says, "Scripture cannot be broken" (John 10:35), and when the apostle Paul says, "All Scripture is breathed out by God" (2 Tim. 3:16), and when the apostle Peter says, the authors of Scripture "were carried along by the Holy Spirit" (2 Pet. 1:21), our heart says *yes*. We have tasted and seen. We know. And the knowing is well founded. We are not leaping in the dark.

Our whole soul resonates with the biblical shout "The sum of your word is truth" (Ps. 119:160). "Forever, O LORD, your word is firmly fixed in the heavens" (Ps. 119:89). "Every word of God proves true" (Prov. 30:5).

When this happens, the whole truth of God washes over us, even in the face of the coronavirus. It comes with incomparable comfort: "When the cares of my heart are many, your consolations cheer my soul" (Ps. 94:19). "The LORD is near to the brokenhearted and saves the crushed in spirit. Many are the afflictions of the righteous, but the LORD delivers him out of them all" (Ps. 34:18–19).

No man can comfort our souls in this pandemic the way God can. His comfort is unshakable. It is the comfort of a great, high Rock in the stormy sea. It comes from his word, the Bible.

Chapter 3

THE ROCK IS RIGHTEOUS

IF GOD IS GOING TO BE OUR ROCK, he must be righteous. An unrighteous Rock is a mirage. The very thing that a global pandemic shakes is our confidence that God is righteous, holy, good. If God is not righteous in the midst of it, we have no Rock.

So we need to ask, What is the holiness and righteousness and goodness of God? Because if we don't know what they are, how will we know if this coronavirus outbreak has made them crumble? Or how will we know if, instead, they are the eternal foundations of the Rock that saves us?

What we will see is that the Bible portrays the holiness, righteousness, and goodness of God not as identical, but as interlocking. We start with God's holiness. What is it?

TRANSCENDENT, INFINITE WORTH

The root meaning of the Old Testament word for holiness is the idea of being separate—different and separated from the ordinary. And when applied to God, this separateness implies that he is in a class by himself. He is like a one-of-a-kind diamond, supremely valuable. We can use the word *transcendent* for this kind of divine separateness. He is so uniquely separate that he transcends all other reality. He is above it and more valuable than all of it.

When Moses struck the rock instead of speaking to it the way God said, God rebuked him: "You did not believe in me, *to uphold me as holy* in the eyes of the people of Israel" (Num. 20:12). In other words, Moses treated God not as exceptional and supremely trustworthy, but as just another human authority along with others that could be ignored.

Or in Isaiah 8:12–13, God said to Isaiah, "Do not fear what [this people] fears, nor be in dread. But the LORD of hosts, him *you shall honor as holy*. Let him be your fear, and let him be your dread." In other words, don't lump God into the same group as all of your ordinary fears and dreads. Treat him as an utterly separate and unique—a transcendent—fear and dread.

Therefore, God's holiness is his infinite transcendence and worth above all else. He is in a class by himself. Which means he doesn't depend on anything else for his existence. He is self-existent. So he needs nothing and depends on nothing. He is complete. Perfect. Therefore, he possesses the greatest value as the source of all reality and all value.

ABOVE ALL BUT NOT SOLITARY

God's infinite height above all other reality does not mean that he is a loveless, solitary mind. The historic doctrine of the Trinity is biblical through and through. God exists as three divine persons. But these three are one—one divine essence. There is one God. Not three. But this one God exists in a mysterious and true unity of Father, Son, and Holy Spirit—each of them eternal and without beginning. Each of them truly God.

So the holiness—the transcendent worth and greatness of God—does not mean he is solitary and loveless in his infinite height. God the Father knows and loves the Son perfectly, completely, infinitely (Mark 1:11; 9:7; Col. 1:13). God the Son knows and loves the Father perfectly, completely, infinitely (John 14:31). The Holy Spirit is the perfect, complete, infinite expression of the Father's and the Son's knowledge and love of each other.

Why does this matter? Because this perfect Trinitarian fellowship is essential to the fullness and perfection and completeness of God. It is essential to his transcendent worth and beauty and greatness—that is, it is essential to his holiness.

HOLINESS IS INTERLOCKING WITH RIGHTEOUSNESS

There is a missing dimension in that description of God's holiness. The Bible speaks of God's holiness not only in terms of transcendence, but also in terms of morality. To be holy is not only to be separate and transcendent, but also to be righteous.

This forces a question that will have great implications for how we view the coronavirus in relation to God: Since righteousness implies doing what is right, and doing what is right implies compliance with some standard of rightness, what standard does God's righteousness comply with?

Before creation, there were no standards outside of God. There was nothing outside of him for him to comply with.

Before creation, God was the only reality. So when there is only God, how do you define what is right for God to do? That is, how can God's holiness encompass not only his transcendence but also his righteousness?

The answer is that the standard of God's righteousness is God. The foundational biblical principle is this: "He cannot deny himself" (2 Tim. 2:13). He cannot act in a way that would deny his own infinite worth and beauty and greatness. This is the standard of what is right for God.

This means that the moral dimension of God's holiness—his righteousness—is his unwavering commitment to act in accord with his worth and beauty and greatness. Every affection, every thought, every word, and every act of God will always be consistent with the infinite worth and beauty of his transcendent fullness. If God were to deny this worth or beauty or greatness, it would not be right. The ultimate standard would be broken. He would be unrighteous.

RIGHTEOUSNESS IS INTERLOCKING WITH GOODNESS

The goodness of God is not identical with his holiness or his righteousness. But it is interlocking in that his holiness overflows in goodness, and his righteousness guides its bestowal. They never contradict each other.

God's goodness is his disposition to be generous—to do what blesses human beings. The transcendent fullness and perfection of God—his holiness—is like a fountain that overflows. This is why he is disposed to be generous. God is not needy. Therefore, he never exploits others to make up for some deficiency in himself. Instead, the impulse of his nature is to give, not get. "He is not served by human hands, as though he needed anything, since he himself gives to all mankind life and breath and everything" (Acts 17:25).

But his goodness is not disconnected from his righteousness. It is not bestowed in a way that would deny his infinite value and beauty and greatness. This is why God's righteousness involves final punishment as well as goodness. When God punishes the unrepentant in hell, he is not bestowing his goodness on them. But he does not cease to be good. His holiness and righteousness govern the bestowal of his goodness.

This is why his goodness flows especially toward those who fear him and take refuge in him. "Oh, how abundant is your goodness, which you have stored up for those who *fear* you and worked for those who *take refuge* in you" (Ps. 31:19).

This reverence and faith do not *earn* God's goodness. Finite, totally dependent sinners can't earn anything from God. God's goodness to sinners is always free and undeserved. Why, then, is God prone to show his abundant goodness to those who fear him and take refuge in him? It's because such reverence and faith display God's worth and beauty and greatness (Rom. 4:20). And, therefore, God's righteousness inclines him to affirm such God-honoring attitudes.

WHAT, THEN, OF THE CORONAVIRUS?

We turn, in the next chapter, to God's all-knowing, all-governing sovereignty over all things. But what we have seen here will keep us from jumping to the conclusion that God's fingers in the coronavirus discredit his holiness or righteousness or goodness. We will not be so naïve as to equate human suffering with divine unrighteousness. Or to conclude that God has ceased to be holy or good when he governs his world.

All of us are sinners. No exceptions. We all have exchanged the glory of God's worth and beauty and greatness for things we enjoy more (Rom. 1:23; 3:23). This is a shameful dishonor to God, whether we feel it or not. We therefore are deserving of punishment. Our dishonoring of God's glory makes us worthy objects of holy wrath. The Bible says we are "by nature children of wrath" (Eph. 2:3). Which means that God would be holy and righteous to withhold his goodness from us.

The coronavirus, therefore, does not point to unholiness or unrighteousness or lack of goodness in God. Our Rock, in these troubled days, is not unrighteous. He is not unholy. "There is none holy like the LORD . . . ; there is no rock like our God" (1 Sam. 2:2). Our Rock is not a mirage.

Chapter 4

SOVEREIGN OVER ALL

IN CHAPTER 2 I USED THE PHRASE "bitter providence." That's what the coronavirus is. To describe some of God's works as bitter is not blasphemy. Naomi, Ruth's mother-in-law, who lost her husband, her two sons, and one daughter-in-law through famine and exile, said:

> The Almighty has dealt very bitterly with me. I went away full, and the LORD has brought me back empty. . . . The Almighty has brought calamity upon me. (Ruth 1:20–21)

She was not lying, overstating, or accusing. It was a simple, and terrible, fact. "Bitter providence" is not a disparagement of God's ways. It's a description.

I also said in chapter 2 that the sweetness of God's word is not diminished in the midst of this bitter providence—not if we have learned the secret of "sorrowful, yet always rejoicing" (2 Cor. 6:10). I said we would come back to this secret. Then I summed it up in a sentence: *The same sovereignty that could stop the coronavirus, yet doesn't, is the very sovereignty that sustains the soul in it.* Knowing this makes all the difference. So is it true?

WHAT GOD WILLS, HE DOES

My aim in this chapter and the next is to show that God is all-governing and all-wise. He is sovereign over the coronavirus. I want to show that this is good news—indeed, it is the secret of experiencing the sweetness of God in his bitter providences.

Saying that God is all-governing means he is sovereign. His sovereignty means that he *can* do, and in fact *does* do, all that he decisively wills to do. I say *decisively* because God, in a sense, wills things he does not carry through. He can express desires that he himself chooses not to act on. In that sense, they are not decisive. He himself does not let such willing or desiring rise to the level of performance.

For example, consider Lamentations 3:32–33:

> Though he cause grief, he will have compassion
>   according to the abundance of his steadfast
>   love;
> for he does not afflict from his heart
>   or grieve the children of men.

He *does* grieve us, but not *from his heart*. I take that to mean that while there are aspects of his character (his heart) that incline away from grieving us, nevertheless other aspects of his character dictate the holiness and righteousness of grieving us.

He is not double-minded. There is a perfect beauty and coherence in how all his attributes cooperate. But neither is he without complexity. His character is more like a symphony than a solo performance.

So when I say that God's sovereignty means that he *can* do, and in fact *does* do, all that he *decisively* wills to do, I mean there is no force outside himself that can thwart or frustrate his will. When he *decides* for a thing to happen, it happens. Or to put it another way, everything happens because God wills it to happen.

ALL-PERVASIVE SOVEREIGNTY

Isaiah teaches that this is part of the very essence of what it means to be God:

> I am God, and there is no other;
>   I am God, and there is none like me,
> declaring the end from the beginning
>   and from ancient times things not yet done,
> saying, "My counsel shall stand,
>   and I will accomplish all my purpose." (Isa. 46:9–10)

To be God is to cause his own counsel to stand—always. God does not just *declare* which future events will happen; he *makes* them happen. He speaks his word, and then he adds, "I am watching over my word to *perform* it" (Jer. 1:12).

Which means, as Job learned from hard experience, "I know that you can do all things, and that no purpose of yours can be thwarted" (Job 42:2). Or as Nebuchadnezzar learned from his merciful humiliation:

> All the inhabitants of the earth are accounted as nothing,
>   and he does according to his will among the host of
>   heaven
>   and among the inhabitants of the earth;

and none can stay his hand
 or say to him, "What have you done?" (Dan. 4:35)

Or as the psalmist says:

Whatever the LORD pleases, he does,
 in heaven and on earth,
 in the seas and all deeps. (Ps. 135:6)

Or as the apostle Paul sums up:

[He] works all things according to the counsel of his will.
(Eph. 1:11)

"All things." Not some things. And "according to *his* will," not according to wills or forces outside himself.

In other words, the sovereignty of God is all-encompassing and all-pervasive. He holds absolute sway over this world. He governs wind (Luke 8:25), lightning (Job 36:32), snow (Ps. 147:16), frogs (Ex. 8:1–15), gnats (Ex. 8:16–19), flies (Ex. 8:20–32), locusts (Ex. 10:1–20), quail (Ex. 16:6–8), worms (Jonah 4:7), fish (Jonah 2:10), sparrows (Matt. 10:29), grass (Ps. 147:8), plants (Jonah 4:6), famine (Ps. 105:16), the sun (Josh. 10:12–13), prison doors (Acts 5:19), blindness (Ex. 4:11; Luke 18:42), deafness (Ex. 4:11; Mark 7:37), paralysis (Luke 5:24–25), fever (Matt. 8:15), every disease (Matt. 4:23), travel plans (James 4:13–15), the hearts of kings (Prov. 21:1; Dan. 2:21), nations (Ps. 33:10), murderers (Acts 4:27–28), and spiritual deadness (Eph. 2:4–5)—and all of them do his sovereign will.

NOT A SEASON FOR SENTIMENTAL VIEWS OF GOD

The coronavirus was sent, therefore, by God. This is not a season for sentimental views of God. It is a bitter season. And God ordained it. God governs it. He will end it. No part of it is outside his sway. Life and death are in his hand.

Job did not sin with his lips (Job 1:22) when he said:

> Naked I came from my mother's womb, and naked shall I return. The LORD gave, and *the LORD has taken away*; blessed be the name of the LORD. (Job 1:21)

The Lord gave. And the Lord took. The Lord took Job's ten children.

In the presence of God, no one has a right to life. Every breath we take is a gift of grace. Every heartbeat, undeserved. Life and death are finally in the hands of God:

> See now that I, even I, am he,
>   and there is no god beside me;
> I kill and I make alive;
>   I wound and I heal;
>   and there is none that can deliver out of
>   my hand. (Deut. 32:39)

Therefore, as we ponder our future with the coronavirus—or any other life-threatening situation—James tells us how to think and speak:

> You ought to say, "If the Lord wills, we will live and do this or that." (James 4:15)

If he wills, we will live. If not, we won't.

For all I know, I will not live to see this book published. I have at least one relative infected with the coronavirus. I am seventy-four years old, and my lungs are compromised with a blood clot and seasonal bronchitis. But these factors do not ultimately decide. God decides. Is that good news? Yes. I'll try to show why in the next chapter.

Chapter 5

THE SWEETNESS OF HIS REIGN

WHY SHOULD I RECEIVE the news of God's sovereignty over the coronavirus, and over my life, as a sweet teaching? The secret, I said, is *knowing that the same sovereignty that could stop the coronavirus, yet doesn't, is the very sovereignty that sustains the soul in it.* In other words, if we try to rescue God from his sovereignty over suffering, we sacrifice his sovereignty to turn all things for good.

GOD'S DETHRONEMENT IS NOT GOOD NEWS

The very sovereignty that rules in sickness is the sovereignty that sustains in loss. The very sovereignty that takes life is the sovereignty that conquered death and brings believers home to heaven and Christ. It is not sweet to think that Satan, sickness, sabotage, fate, or chance has the last say in my life. That is *not* good news.

That God reigns is good news. Why? Because God is holy and righteous and good. And he is infinitely wise. "With God are wisdom and might; he has counsel and understanding" (Job 12:13). "His understanding is beyond measure" (Ps. 147:5). "Oh, the depth of the riches and wisdom and knowledge of God!" (Rom. 11:33). His great aim is that "the manifold wisdom of God might now be made known to the rulers and authorities in the heavenly places" (Eph. 3:10).

Nothing surprises him, confuses him, or baffles him. His infinite power rests in the hands of infinite holiness and righteousness and goodness—and wisdom. And all of that stands in the service of those who trust his Son, Jesus Christ. What God did in sending Jesus to die for sinners has everything to do with the coronavirus.

HOW GOD SECURED "ALL THINGS" FOR SINNERS

Here's the connection. It's Romans 8:32: "He who did not spare his own Son but gave him up for us all, how will he not also with him graciously give us all things?" This means that God's willingness to send his Son to be crucified in our place is his declaration and validation that he will use all his sovereignty to "give us all things." "How will he not also with him graciously give us *all things*?" Meaning: he most certainly will. It is guaranteed by the blood of his Son.

And what are these "all things"? They are the things we need to do his will, glorify his name, and make it safely into his joyful presence.

Three verses later, Paul explains how it works in real life—in the coronavirus. What does it look like when God's infinite, blood-certified commitment to give us "all things" meets the coronavirus? Here's what he says:

> Who shall separate us from the love of Christ? Shall tribulation, or distress, or persecution, or famine, or nakedness, or danger, or sword [or the coronavirus]? As it is written,
>
> > "For your sake we are being killed all the day long;
> > we are regarded as sheep to be slaughtered."
>
> No, in all these things we are more than conquerors through him who loved us. (Rom. 8:35–37)

Don't miss these painful and amazing words: "We are being killed all the day long." That means that the "all things" God will give to us, because he did not spare his Son, includes bringing us safely through death. Or as he says in Romans 8:38–39, "I am sure that neither death nor life . . . will be able to separate us from the love of God in Christ Jesus our Lord."

WHAT SATAN MEANS FOR EVIL

Even if Satan, on his divine leash, has a hand in our suffering and death, he is not ultimate. He cannot hurt us without God's permission and limitation (Job 1:12; Luke 22:31; 2 Cor. 12:7). And in the end, it is right for us to say to Satan what Joseph said to his brothers who had sold him into slavery: "As for you, you meant evil against me, but God meant it for good" (Gen. 50:20).

Be careful not to water this down. It does *not* say, "God *used* it for good" or "God *turned* it for good." It says, "God *meant* it for good." They had an evil purpose. God had a good purpose. God didn't start cleaning up halfway through this sinful affair. He had a purpose, a meaning, from the beginning. From the start, he meant it for good.

This is the key to comfort when the evil of men and the evil of Satan compound our suffering. In Christ, we have every right to say to Satan (or to evil men), "You meant it for evil. But God meant it for good." Neither Satan nor sickness nor sinful man is sovereign. Only God is. And he is good—and wise and sovereign.

NOT A SPARROW, EVERY HAIR

Jesus expresses the sweetness of God's sovereignty for his disciples as beautifully as anyone:

> Are not two sparrows sold for a penny? And not one of them will fall to the ground apart from your Father. But even the hairs of your head are all numbered. Fear not, therefore; you are of more value than many sparrows. (Matt. 10:29–31)

Not one sparrow falls but by God's plan. Not one virus moves but by God's plan. This is meticulous sovereignty. And what does Jesus say next? Three things: You are of more value than many sparrows. The hairs of your head are all numbered. Fear not.

Why not? Because God's meticulous sovereignty—whether we live or die—serves his holiness and righteousness and goodness and wisdom. In Christ we are not his dispensable pawns. We are his valued children. "You are of more value than many sparrows."

This is the secret mentioned earlier: *knowing that the same sovereignty that could stop the coronavirus, yet doesn't, is the very sovereignty that sustains the soul in it.* And not only sustains, but sees to it that everything, bitter and sweet, works together for our good—the good of those who love God and are called in Christ (Rom. 8:28–30).

IMMORTAL TILL MY WORK IS DONE

That kind of rock-solid confidence in the face of death has emboldened Christ's people for two thousand years. The truth of God's wise and good sovereignty has been the stabilizing power for thousands of Christians in the sacrifices of love.

For example, Henry Martyn, missionary to India and Persia, who died of the plague (like the coronavirus) when he was thirty-one (October 16, 1812), wrote in his journal in January 1812:

> To all appearance, the present year will be more perilous than any I have seen; but if I live to complete the Persian

New Testament, my life after that will be of less importance.
But whether life or death be mine, may Christ be magnified
in me! If he has work for me to do, I cannot die.[2]

This has often been paraphrased as "I am immortal till
Christ's work for me to do is done." This is profoundly
true. And it rests squarely on the reality that life and death
are in the hands of our sovereign God. Indeed, the entire
cause of Christ is in his hand. Seven years earlier, Martyn,
at age twenty-four, had written:

Were God not the sovereign of the universe, how miserable
I should be! But the Lord reigneth, let the earth be glad.
And Christ's cause shall prevail. O my soul, be happy in
the prospect.[3]

Part 2

WHAT IS GOD DOING THROUGH THE CORONAVIRUS?

PRELIMINARY THOUGHTS:
SEEING AND POINTING

IF GOD HAS NOT BEEN DETHRONED, if, indeed, he governs "all things according to the counsel of his will" (Eph. 1:11), and if this coronavirus outbreak, with all its devastation, is in his holy, righteous, good, and wise hands, then what is he doing? What are his purposes?

STOP REGARDING MAN

The first thing to say, before trying to answer this question, is that, compared to the wisdom of God, my opinion counts for nothing. So does yours. What we think, out of our own heads, is of little significance. The Bible says that "whoever trusts in his own mind is a fool" (Prov. 28:26). Instead, we are told, "Trust in the LORD with all your heart, and do not lean on your own understanding" (Prov. 3:5).

We humans are finite, sinful, culturally conditioned, and shaped (and misshaped) by our genes and personal history. Out of our hearts and minds and mouths come every manner of self-justifying rationalization for our own preferences. So we would be wise to pay attention to the prophet Isaiah when he says, "Stop regarding man in whose nostrils is breath, for of what account is he?" (Isa. 2:22).

Is it, then, not presumption for me to write this book, let alone a section titled, "What Is God Doing through the Coronavirus"?

No. It is not presumptuous. Not if God has spoken in the Christian Scriptures. Not if God has stooped to speak in human words so that we might truly (though partially) know him and his ways. Not if Paul's words are true: "[God] lavished [his grace] upon us, in all wisdom and insight, making known to us the mystery of his will" (Eph. 1:8–9). Not if, as Paul says, "*by reading* you can perceive my insight into the mystery of Christ" (Eph. 3:4, my translation).

God is not silent about what he is doing in this world. He has given us the Scriptures. In chapter 2, I pointed to some of the reasons we may trust the Bible as God's word. So my aim is not to dream up ideas about what God might be doing. My aim is to listen to his word in Scripture and commend to you what I hear.

HOW INSCRUTABLE HIS WAYS

Another thing I should say before I try to answer the question, What is God doing? is that he is always doing a billion things we do not know:

> You have multiplied, O LORD my God,
>> your wondrous deeds and your thoughts toward us;
>> none can compare with you!
> I will proclaim and tell of them,
>> yet they are more than can be told. (Ps. 40:5)

Not only are his designs in the coronavirus beyond counting; they are, in many ways, inscrutable. "Oh, the depth of the riches and wisdom and knowledge of God! How unsearchable are his judgments and how inscrutable his ways!" (Rom. 11:33). But when Paul wrote that, he was not saying, "So close your Bible and make up your own reality."

On the contrary, those words about God's inscrutable ways were written as a climax to eleven chapters of the greatest news in the world, all of which are written to be understood. For example, when Paul touches on the inevitability of suffering, he says:

> We rejoice in our sufferings, *knowing* that suffering produces endurance, and endurance produces character, and character produces hope, and hope does not put us to shame, because God's love has been poured into our hearts through the Holy Spirit. (Rom. 5:3–5)

"Knowing"! The Scriptures are written that we might *know* the things God has revealed. Especially about suffering—including this coronavirus outbreak. So *inscrutable* means that God is always doing more than we can see—and even what we can see, we would not have seen if he had not revealed it.

POINTING TO REALITY

So my job here is not to imagine, as in John Lennon's famous song.[4] He tells us to imagine that there's no heaven, no hell, but only sky. And then he says that such imagining is easy. Just try. Right. It *is* easy. Way too easy. The coronavirus demands hard reality, not easy imaginings. God and his word are the reality we need—the Rock under our feet. So my aim here is to point to reality, not create reality. My aim is to hear what God has said, and affirm rather than imagine.

I will point to what the Bible teaches and then make the connections with the coronavirus. Yours is to judge what is right.

I say that because it's what Jesus said about "interpreting the present time." He was indignant that people could use their reason to make sense out of weather patterns but not the divine working of God in history:

> You hypocrites! You know how to interpret the appearance of earth and sky, but why do you not know how to interpret the present time? And why do you not judge for yourselves what is right? (Luke 12:56–57)

So my hope is that you will ask for God's help, look to God's word, and judge for yourselves what is right. I hope you will test what I say by the Scriptures (1 John 4:1), and hold fast to what is good (1 Thess. 5:21).

SIX PATHS TO FOLLOW

Many pages could be written about each of the six answers I am going to give to the question, What is God doing through the coronavirus? But with the urgency of the hour, I won't take time for that. I will only point to paths of biblical truth that I hope you will pursue after you close this book. I wish we could walk far down those paths together. But I must leave that with you. May God guide you.

What is God doing through the coronavirus?

Chapter 6

PICTURING MORAL HORROR

ANSWER 1.

God is giving the world in the coronavirus
outbreak, as in all other calamities,
a physical picture of the moral horror and
spiritual ugliness of God-belittling sin.

SIN, IN FACT, IS WHY all physical misery exists. The third chapter of the Bible describes the entrance of sin into the world. It shows sin to be the origin of global devastation and misery (Gen. 3:1–19). Paul summed it up in Romans 5:12: "Sin came into the world through one man, and death through sin, and so death spread to all men because all sinned."

The world has been broken ever since. All its beauty is interwoven with evil and disasters and diseases and frustrations. God had created it perfect. "God saw everything that he had made, and behold, it was very good" (Gen. 1:31). But from humanity's fall into sin to this very day, history, for all its wonders, is a conveyor belt of corpses.

THE FALL IS JUDGMENT

The Bible does not see this brokenness as merely natural, but as the judgment of God on a world permeated with sin. Here's how Paul described the effects of God's judgment on the world because of sin:

> The creation was subjected to futility, not willingly, but because of him who subjected it, in hope that the creation itself will be set free from its bondage to corruption and obtain the freedom of the glory of the children of God. For we know that the whole creation has been groaning together in the pains of childbirth until now. (Rom. 8:20–22)

Futility. Bondage to corruption. Groaning. These are images of global devastation and misery since sin entered the world. And Paul says this devastation is owing to the

judgment of God: "The creation *was subjected* to futility
. . . because of him who *subjected it* in hope" (8:20). Satan
did not subject it *in hope*. Adam did not subject it *in hope*.
God did. As Paul said in Romans 5:16, "The judgment
following one trespass brought condemnation."

EVEN HIS CHILDREN UNDER JUDGMENT

To be sure, this passage is full of hope—"the freedom of
the glory of the children of God" (Rom. 8:21). God has
a stunning plan for a new creation, where "he will wipe
away every tear from their eyes" (Rev. 21:4). But for now,
we are all under his judgment. He has subjected the world
to death, disaster, and misery.

Yes, even his own children—those whom he "predestined
. . . for adoption" (Eph. 1:5), redeemed by the blood of his
Son (Eph. 1:7), and appointed for eternal life (Eph. 1:18)—
even we suffer and die because of God's judgment in the
fall. "We ourselves, who have the firstfruits of the Spirit,
groan inwardly as we wait eagerly for adoption as sons,
the redemption of our bodies" (Rom. 8:23). *Christians* get
swept away in tsunamis. *Christians* are killed in terrorist
attacks. *Christians* get the coronavirus.

PURIFICATION, NOT PUNISHMENT

The difference for Christians—those who embrace Christ as their supreme treasure—is that our experience of this corruption is not condemnation. "There is therefore now no condemnation for those who are in Christ" (Rom. 8:1). The pain for us is purifying, not punitive.

"God has not destined us for wrath" (1 Thess. 5:9). We die of disease and disaster like all humans. But for those who are in Christ, the "sting" of death has been removed (1 Cor. 15:55). "To die is gain" (Phil. 1:21). To depart is to "be with Christ" (Phil. 1:23).

SATAN IS REAL—AND RESTRICTED

When I trace the miseries of this world back to God's judgment, I am not shutting my eyes to the fact that Satan is very involved in our global misery. The Bible calls him "the god of this world" (2 Cor. 4:4), and "the ruler of this world" (John 12:31), and "the prince of the power of the air" (Eph. 2:2). He has been "a murderer from the beginning" (John 8:44). He binds and oppresses with many diseases (Luke 13:16; Acts 10:38).

But Satan is on a leash. The leash is in God's hands. He

does not act without God's leave. He acts only with permission and limitation (Job 1:12; 2:6; Luke 22:31; 2 Cor. 12:7). God decides finally the extent of Satan's damage. He is not separate from God's judgment. He serves it—unwittingly.

KEY QUESTION

Now here is the question that brings the meaning of the coronavirus into sharper focus. Why did God bring a *physical* judgment on the world for a *moral* evil? Adam and Eve defied God. Their hearts turned against God. They preferred their own wisdom to his. They chose independence over trust. This *defying* and *preferring* and *choosing* was a spiritual and moral evil. It was sin in the *soul* first, not in the body. It was first Godward, not manward.

But in response to moral and spiritual rebellion, God subjected the *physical* world to disaster and misery. Why? Why not leave the physical world in good order and bring misery on the human soul, since that's where it all started?

AN ANSWER

Here's my suggestion: God put the physical world under a curse so that the physical horrors we see around us in diseases and calamities would become a vivid picture of how horrible sin is. In other words, *physical evil is a parable, a drama, a signpost pointing to the moral outrage of rebellion against God.*

Why might that be fitting? Because in our present condition, after the fall, blinded by sin, we cannot see or feel how repugnant sin against God is. Hardly anyone in the world feels the horror of preferring other things over God. Who loses any sleep over our daily belittling of God by neglect and defiance?

But, oh, how we feel our physical pain! How indignant we can become if God touches our bodies! We may not grieve over the way we demean God every day in our hearts. But let the coronavirus come and threaten our bodies, and he has our attention. Or does he? *Physical pain is God's trumpet blast to tell us that something is dreadfully wrong in the world.* Disease and deformity are God's pictures in the *physical* realm of what sin is like in the *spiritual* realm.

And that is true, even though some of the most godly people in the world bear those diseases and deformities. Calamities are God's previews of what sin deserves and will one day receive in judgment a thousand times worse. They are warnings. They are wake-up calls to see the moral horror and spiritual ugliness of sin against God.

Would that we could all see and feel how repugnant, how offensive, how abominable it is to treat our Maker with contempt, to ignore him and distrust him and demean him and give him less attention in our hearts than we give the style of our hair.

We need to see this, and feel this, or we will not turn to Christ for salvation from the ugliness of sin. We may cry out to escape the *penalty* of sin. But will we see and hate the God-demeaning, moral *ugliness* of sin? If we don't, it will not be because God has not provided vivid portrayals of it in physical misery—like the coronavirus. Therefore, God is mercifully shouting to us in these days: Wake up! Sin against God is like this! It is horrible and ugly. And far more dangerous than the coronavirus.

Chapter 7

SENDING SPECIFIC DIVINE JUDGMENTS

ANSWER 2.

Some people will be infected with the corona-
virus as a specific judgment from God because
of their sinful attitudes and actions.

THE FACT THAT ALL MISERY is a result of the fall—a result of the entrance of God-diminishing sin into the world—does not mean that all individual suffering is a specific judgment for personal sins. For example, Job's suffering was not owing to his particular sins. The very first sentence of that book makes this clear: "Job . . . was blameless and upright, one who feared God and turned away from evil" (Job 1:1).

And as we saw earlier, God's own people experience many of the physical effects of his judgment. The apostle Peter put it like this:

> It is time for judgment to begin *at the household of God*; and if it begins *with us*, what will be the outcome for those who do not obey the gospel of God? And "If the righteous is scarcely saved, what will become of the ungodly and the sinner?" (1 Pet. 4:17–18)

For "the household of God," this judgment from God is *purifying*, not *punitive*—not punishment. So not all suffering is owing to the specific judgments of God on specific sins. Nevertheless, God sometimes uses disease to bring particular judgments upon those who reject him and give themselves over to sin.

EXAMPLES OF SPECIFIC JUDGMENTS ON SPECIFIC SINS

I'll give two examples of specific judgments on specific sins.

In Acts 12, Herod the king exalted himself by allowing himself to be called a god. "Immediately an angel of the

Lord struck him down, because he did not give God the glory, and he was eaten by worms and breathed his last" (Acts 12:23). God can do that with all who exalt themselves. Which means we should be amazed that more of our rulers do not drop dead every day because of their arrogance before God and man. God's restraint is a great mercy.

Another example is the sin of homosexual intercourse. In Romans 1:27, the apostle Paul says, "Men likewise gave up natural relations with women and were consumed with passion for one another, men committing shameless acts with men and receiving in themselves the due penalty for their error." That "due penalty" is the painful effect "in themselves" of their sin.

This "due penalty" is just one example of the judgment of God that we see in Romans 1:18, where it says, "The wrath of God is revealed from heaven against all ungodliness and unrighteousness of men, who by their unrighteousness suppress the truth." Therefore, while not all suffering is a specific judgment for specific sins, some is.

LET EVERY SOUL BE SEARCHED

The coronavirus is, therefore, never a clear and simple punishment on any person. The most loving, Spirit-filled Christian, whose sins are forgiven through Christ, may die of the coronavirus disease. But it is fitting that every one of us search our own heart to discern if our suffering is God's judgment on the way we live.

If we come to Christ, we can know that our suffering is not the punitive judgment of God. We can know this because Jesus said, "Whoever hears my word and believes him who sent me has eternal life. *He does not come into judgment*, but has passed from death to life" (John 5:24). There is no condemnation for those who are in Christ Jesus (Rom. 8:1). It is discipline, not destruction. "For the Lord disciplines the one he loves, and chastises every son whom he receives" (Heb. 12:6).

Chapter 8

AWAKENING US FOR THE SECOND COMING

ANSWER 3.

The coronavirus is a God-given wake-up call to be ready for the second coming of Christ.

EVEN THOUGH THE HISTORY of the Christian church is littered with failed predictions of the end of the world, it remains true that Jesus Christ is coming back. "Men of Galilee," the angel said at Jesus's departure, "why do you stand looking into heaven? This Jesus, who was taken up from you into heaven, will come in the same way as you saw him go into heaven" (Acts 1:11).

At his coming, he will judge the world:

> When the Son of Man comes in his glory, and all the angels with him, then he will sit on his glorious throne. Before him will be gathered all the nations, and he will separate people one from another as a shepherd separates the sheep from the goats. (Matt. 25:31–32)

For those who are not ready to meet Christ, that day will come suddenly like a trap:

> Watch yourselves lest your hearts be weighed down with dissipation and drunkenness and cares of this life, and that day come upon you suddenly like a trap. (Luke 21:34)

BIRTH PAINS

Jesus said there would be pointers to his coming—like wars, famines, and earthquakes (Matt. 24:7). He called these signs "birth pains" (Matt. 24:8). The image is of the earth as a woman in labor, trying to give birth to the new world, which Jesus would bring into being at his coming.

Paul picked up this imagery in Romans 8:22 and referred the birth pains to *all* the groanings of this age—all the miseries of disaster and disease (like the coronavirus).

He pictured us in our diseases as part of the labor pains of the world. We groan as we wait for the redemption of our bodies at the coming of Jesus, when he will raise the dead and gives us new, glorious bodies (Phil. 3:21):

> The creation itself will be set free from its bondage to corruption and obtain the freedom of the glory of the children of God. For we know that the whole creation has been groaning together in *the pains of childbirth* until now. And not only the creation, but we ourselves, who have the firstfruits of the Spirit, groan inwardly as we wait eagerly for adoption as sons, the redemption of our bodies. (Rom. 8:21–23)

STAY AWAKE!

My point is this: Jesus wants us to see the birth pains (including the coronavirus) as reminders and alerts that he is coming and that we need to be ready. "You . . . must be ready, for the Son of Man is coming at an hour you do not expect" (Matt. 24:44).

You don't have to be a date setter in order take seriously what Jesus says. And what he says is unmistakable: "Be on guard, *keep awake*. For you do not know when the time will come. . . . *Stay awake*—for you do not know when the master of the house will come. . . . And what I say to you, I say to all: *Stay awake*" (Mark 13:33–37).

The message is clear. Stay awake. Stay awake. Stay awake. And the birth pains of the natural world are meant for this message. But, oh, how many people are not awake! For all their frenzied activity, they are sound asleep in regard to the coming of Jesus Christ. The peril is great. And the coronavirus is a merciful wake-up call to be ready.

The way to be ready is to come to Jesus Christ, receive forgiveness for sins, and walk in his light. Then you will be among those who

> are not in darkness for that day to surprise you like a thief. For you are all children of light. . . . So then . . . let us keep awake. . . . For God has not destined us for wrath, but to obtain salvation through our Lord Jesus Christ, who died for us so that whether we are awake or asleep we might live with him. (1 Thess. 5:4–10)

Chapter 9

REALIGNING US WITH
THE INFINITE WORTH OF CHRIST

ANSWER 4.

*The coronavirus is God's thunderclap call
for all of us to repent and realign our lives
with the infinite worth of Christ.*

THE CORONAVIRUS IS NOT UNIQUE as a call to repentance. In fact, all natural disasters—whether floods,
famines, locusts, tsunamis, or diseases—are God's painful
and merciful summons to repent.

We see this from the way Jesus responds to disaster in
Luke 13:1–5:

> There were some present at that very time who told him
> about the Galileans whose blood Pilate had mingled with
> their sacrifices. And he answered them, "Do you think
> that these Galileans were worse sinners than all the other
> Galileans, because they suffered in this way? No, I tell you;
> but unless you repent, you will all likewise perish. Or those
> eighteen on whom the tower in Siloam fell and killed them:
> do you think that they were worse offenders than all the
> others who lived in Jerusalem? No, I tell you; but unless
> you repent, you will all likewise perish.

Pilate had slaughtered worshipers in the temple. The tower
in Siloam had collapsed and killed eighteen bystanders. One
disaster was the fruit of human wickedness. The other was
apparently an accident.

THE MEANING OF CALAMITY—FOR YOU

The crowds want to know from Jesus, "What's the meaning
of this? Was it an act of God's specific judgment on specific
sins?" Jesus's answer is amazing. He draws a meaning from
these disasters that relates to everyone, not just the ones who
died. In both cases, he says, "No, those who were murdered
by Pilate and those who were crushed under the tower were
not worse sinners than—you."

You? Why does he bring up *their* sin? They weren't asking for his opinion about their *own* sin. They were curious about the others. They wanted to know what the disasters meant for the victims, not for the rest of us.

That's what makes Jesus's answer amazing. In essence, he said that the meaning of these disasters is for *everyone*. And the message is "Repent, or perish." He says it twice: "Unless you repent, you will all likewise perish" (Luke 13:3). "Unless you repent, you will all likewise perish" (13:5).

MERCIFUL CALL WHILE THERE'S TIME

What was Jesus doing? He was redirecting the people's astonishment. The astonishment that prompted these folks to query Jesus is misplaced. They were astonished that people were murdered so cruelly and crushed so meaninglessly. But Jesus says, "What you ought to be astonished at is that *you* were not the ones murdered and crushed. In fact, if you don't repent, you yourselves will meet a judgment like that someday."

From this, I infer that God has a merciful message in all such disasters. The message is that we are all sinners, bound for destruction, and disasters are a gracious summons from

God to repent and be saved while there is still time. Jesus turned from the dead to the living and essentially said, "Let's not talk about the dead; let's talk about *you*. This is more urgent. What happened to them is about *you*. Your biggest issue is not *their* sin but *your* sin." I think that's God's message for the world in this coronavirus outbreak. He is calling the world to repentance while there's still time.

WHAT DOES *REPENTANCE* MEAN?

Let's be more specific. What does *repentance* mean? The word in the New Testament means a change of heart and mind. Not a superficial change of opinion, but a deep transformation so that we perceive and prize God and Jesus for who they really are. Jesus described the change like this:

> You shall love the Lord your God with all your heart and with all your soul and with all your mind. (Matt. 22:37)

> Whoever loves father or mother more than me is not worthy of me, and whoever loves son or daughter more than me is not worthy of me. (Matt. 10:37)

In other words, the most fundamental change of heart and mind that repentance calls for is to treasure God with all that you are and to treasure Jesus more than all other relations.

WHY WOULD JESUS THREATEN US WITH PERISHING?

The reason Jesus said that we all likewise would perish if we don't repent is that we all have exchanged the treasure that God is for lesser things we love more (Rom. 1:22–23), and we all have treated Jesus as less desirable than money and entertainment and friends and family. The reason all of us deserve to perish is not a list of rules we have broken, but an infinite value we have scorned—the infinite value of all that God is for us in Jesus Christ.

WAKING UP TO OUR SUICIDAL PREFERENCES

Repentance means waking up from the suicidal preference of tin over gold, foundations of sand over solid rock, games in the gutter over a holiday at the sea. As C. S. Lewis writes:

> We are half-hearted creatures, fooling about with drink and sex and ambition when *infinite joy* is offered us, like an ignorant child who wants to go on making mud pies in a slum because he cannot imagine what is meant by the offer of a holiday at the sea. We are far too easily pleased.[5]

The "infinite joy" Lewis mentions is the experience of seeing and savoring and sharing the worth and beauty and greatness of Christ.

ROUSED TO RELY ON CHRIST

What God is doing in the coronavirus is showing us—graphically, painfully—that nothing in this world gives the security and satisfaction that we find in the infinite greatness and worth of Jesus. This global pandemic takes away our freedom of movement, our business activity, and our face-to-face relations. It takes away our security and our comfort. And, in the end, it may take away our lives.

The reason God exposes us to such losses is to rouse us to rely on Christ. Or to put it another way, the reason he makes calamity the occasion for offering Christ to the world is that the supreme, all-satisfying greatness of Christ shines more brightly when Christ sustains joy in suffering.

GIFT OF DESPERATION

Consider, for example, why God brought Paul to the point where he despaired of life:

> We do not want you to be unaware, brothers, of the affliction we experienced in Asia. For we were so utterly burdened beyond our strength that we despaired of life itself. Indeed, we felt that we had received the sentence of death. But that was to make us rely not on ourselves but on God who raises the dead. (2 Cor. 1:8–9)

Paul does not view this experience of desperation as satanic or random. It is purposeful. And God is the one whose purpose is mentioned: this life-threatening experience "was to make us rely not on ourselves but on God who raises the dead" (1:9).

This is the message of the coronavirus: Stop relying on yourselves and turn to God. You cannot even *stop* death. God can *raise* the dead. And of course "relying on God" does not mean that Christians become do-nothings. Christians have never been do-nothings. It means that the ground, the pattern, and the goal of all our doings is God. As Paul said, "I worked harder than any of them, though it was not I, but the grace of God that is with me" (1 Cor. 15:10).

The coronavirus calls us to make God the all-important, pervasive reality in our lives. Our lives depend on him more than they depend on breath. And sometimes God takes our breath in order to throw us onto himself.

THE MEANING OF THORNS

Or consider God's purpose in Paul's painful thorn in the flesh:

> To keep me from becoming conceited because of the surpassing greatness of the revelations, a thorn was given me in the flesh, a messenger of Satan to harass me, to keep me from becoming conceited. Three times I pleaded with the Lord about this, that it should leave me. But he said to me, "My grace is sufficient for you, for my power is made perfect in weakness." Therefore I will boast all the more gladly of my weaknesses, so that the power of Christ may rest upon me. (2 Cor. 12:7–9)

Paul was blessed with great revelations. God saw the danger of pride. Satan saw the danger of truth and joy. God governs Satan's strategy so that what Satan thinks will ruin Paul's witness actually serves Paul's humility and gladness. Paul gets a thorn in the flesh—a "messenger of Satan." And a messenger of God! We don't know what the thorn is. But we know that thorns are painful. And we know that Paul asked three times that Christ would take it away.

But Christ will not. He has a purpose for this pain. Namely, "My power is made perfect in weakness" (12:9).

His purpose is that through Paul's unwavering faith and joy, Christ would shine as more valuable than health. Paul's response to this purpose? "I will boast all the more *gladly* of my weaknesses" (12:9).

Gladly! How can this be? Why is Paul willing to embrace his thorn with gladness? Because his greatest goal in life is that Christ be magnified in his body whether by life or by death (Phil. 1:20). To see the beauty of Christ, to cherish Christ as his supreme treasure, to show Christ to the world as better than health and life—that was Paul's joy. A beautiful poem called "The Thorn," by Martha Snell Nicholson (1898–1953), ends like this:

> I learned He never gives a thorn without this added grace,
> He takes the thorn to pin aside the veil which hides
>   His face.

IN LOSS, GAIN

Paul embraced loss, in part, because in the loss, Christ was more fully gain:

> Indeed, I count everything as loss because of the surpassing worth of knowing Christ Jesus my Lord. For his sake I have

> suffered the loss of all things and count them as rubbish, in order that I may gain Christ. (Phil. 3:8)

This is what it means to repent: to experience a change of heart and mind that treasures God in Christ more than life. "Because your steadfast love is *better than life*, my lips will praise you" (Ps. 63:3). This was Paul's faith. It was true in life and death. In life, because Christ is the sweetness of every pleasure, and better than them all. And in death, because "in [God's] presence there is fullness of joy; at [his] right hand are pleasures forevermore" (Ps. 16:11).

The coronavirus pandemic is the experience of loss—from the smallest loss of convenience to the greatest loss of life. And if we know the secret of Paul's joy, we may experience the loss as gain. That is what God is saying to the world. Repent and realign your life with the infinite worth of Christ.

Chapter 10

CREATING GOOD WORKS IN DANGER

ANSWER 5.

The coronavirus is God's call to his people to overcome self-pity and fear, and with courageous joy, to do the good works of love that glorify God.

JESUS TAUGHT HIS FOLLOWERS to "let your light shine before others, so that they may see your good works and give glory to your Father who is in heaven" (Matt. 5:16). What is often not noticed is that being the salt of the earth and the light of the world in this way was the more salty and the more bright because the good deeds were to be done even in the midst of suffering.

BRIGHTNESS IN THE DARKNESS OF DANGER

Jesus has just said, "Blessed are you when others revile you and persecute you and utter all kinds of evil against you falsely on my account. Rejoice and be glad, for your reward is great in heaven" (Matt. 5:11–12). Then, without a break, he says, "You are the salt of the earth. . . . You are the light of the world" (Matt. 5:13–16).

It is not mere good deeds that give Christianity its tang and luster. It is good deeds in spite of danger. Many non-Christians do good deeds. But seldom do people give glory to God because of them.

Yes, the danger in Matthew 5 was persecution, not disease. But the principle holds. Deeds of love in the context of danger, whether disease or persecution, point more clearly to the fact that these deeds are sustained by hope in God. For example, Jesus says:

> When you give a feast, invite the poor, the crippled, the lame, the blind, and you will be blessed, because they cannot repay you. For you will be repaid at the resurrection of the just. (Luke 14:13–14)

Hope in God beyond death ("you will be repaid at the resurrection") sustains and empowers good deeds that hold no prospect for reward in this life. The same would hold true for good deeds that put us in danger, especially the danger of death.

HOW PETER APPLIED JESUS'S TEACHING

The apostle Peter, more than any other New Testament writer, picks up the explicit teaching of Jesus about good deeds:

> Keep your conduct among the Gentiles honorable, so that when they speak against you as evildoers, they may see your good deeds and glorify God on the day of visitation. (1 Pet. 2:12)

And Peter makes the same point about good deeds in the face of danger. He says, "Let those who suffer according to God's will entrust their souls to a faithful Creator while doing good" (1 Pet. 4:19). In other words, don't let the possibility, or the reality, of suffering stop you from doing good deeds.

CHRIST DIED TO CREATE GOOD DEEDS IN DANGER

Peter links this new kind of life with the death of Jesus for our sins: "[Christ] himself bore our sins in his body on the tree, that we might die to sin and *live to righteousness*" (1 Pet. 2:24). Because of Christ, Christians put sin to death and pour themselves into the good deeds of righteousness.

Paul makes the same connection between the death of Jesus and the zeal of Christians for good works: "[Christ] gave himself for us to redeem us from all lawlessness and to purify for himself a people for his own possession who are *zealous for good works*" (Titus 2:14).

Paul also makes it plain that these good works are aimed at both Christians and non-Christians. "As we have opportunity, let us do good *to everyone*, and especially to those who are of the household of faith" (Gal. 6:10). "See that no one repays anyone evil for evil, but always seek to do good to one another *and to everyone*" (1 Thess. 5:15).

CHRIST MAGNIFIED IN RISKY KINDNESS

The ultimate aim of God for his people is that we glorify his greatness and magnify the worth of his Son, Jesus Christ. "Whether you eat or drink, or whatever you do, do all to the glory of God" (1 Cor. 10:31). "It is my eager expectation and hope that . . . Christ will be magnified in my body, whether by life or by death" (Phil. 1:20, my translation).

God glorified in everything. Christ magnified in life and death. This is the great, God-given goal of human life.

Therefore, one of God's purposes in the coronavirus is that his people put to death self-pity and fear, and give themselves to good deeds in the presence of danger. Christians lean toward need, not comfort. Toward love, not safety. That's what our Savior is like. That is what he died for.

EXAMPLE OF THE EARLY CHURCH

Rodney Stark, in his book *The Triumph of Christianity*, points out that in the first centuries of the Christian church the "truly revolutionary principle was that Christian love and charity must extend beyond the boundaries of family and even those of faith, to all in need."[6]

Two great plagues struck the Roman Empire in AD 165 and 251. Outside of the Christian church, there was no cultural or religious foundation for mercy and sacrifice. "There was no belief that the gods cared about human affairs."[7] And "mercy was regarded as a character defect and pity as a pathological emotion: because mercy involves providing *unearned* help or relief, it is contrary to justice."[8]

Therefore, while a third of the empire was perishing

from disease, physicians fled to their country estates. Those with symptoms were cast out of homes. Priests forsook the temples. But Stark observes, "Christians claimed to have answers and, most of all, they took appropriate actions."[9]

The *answers* included the forgiveness of sins through Christ and the hope of eternal life beyond death. This was a precious message in a season of medical helplessness and utter hopelessness.

As for the *actions*, large numbers of Christians cared for the sick and the dying. Toward the end of the second plague, Bishop Dionysius of Alexandria wrote a letter, extolling the members of his church:

> Most of our brothers showed unbounded love and loyalty, never sparing themselves and thinking only of one another. Heedless of danger, they took charge of the sick, attending to their every need and ministering to them in Christ, and with them departed this life serenely happy.[10]

PUTTING TO SILENCE THE IGNORANCE OF EMPERORS

Over time, this countercultural, Christ-sustained care for the sick and the poor had the effect of winning many people away from the surrounding paganism. Two centuries later, when the Roman emperor Julian (AD 332–363) wanted to breathe new life back into the ancient Roman religion and saw Christianity as a growing threat, he wrote, in frustration, to the Roman high priest of Galatia:

> Atheism [i.e., Christian faith] has been specially advanced through the loving service rendered to strangers, and through their care for the burial of the dead. It is a scandal that there is not a single Jew who is a beggar, and that the godless Galileans [i.e., Christians] care not only for their own poor but for ours as well; while those who belong to us look in vain for the help that we should render them.[11]

RELIEVING GOD-SENT SUFFERING

There is no contradiction between seeing the coronavirus as God's act and calling Christians to take risks to alleviate the suffering that it causes. Ever since God subjected the world to sin and misery at the fall, he has ordained that his people seek to rescue the perishing, even though he is the one who has appointed the judgment of perishing. God himself came into the world in Jesus Christ to rescue people from his own just judgment (Rom. 5:9). That is what the cross of Christ means.

Therefore, the good deeds of God's people will include prayers for the healing of the sick and for God to stay his hand and turn back the pandemic, and that he would provide a cure. We pray about the coronavirus, and we work to alleviate its suffering the way Abraham Lincoln prayed for the end of the Civil War, and worked to end it, even though he saw it as a judgment from God:

> Fondly do we hope—fervently do we pray—that this mighty scourge of war may speedily pass away. Yet, if God wills that it continue, until all the wealth piled by the bond-man's two hundred and fifty years of unrequited toil shall be sunk, and until every drop of blood drawn with the lash, shall be paid by another drawn with the sword, as was said three thousand years ago, so still it must be said "the judgments of the Lord are true and righteous altogether."

God has his work to do—much of it secret. We have ours. If we trust him and obey his word, he will cause his sovereignty and our service to accomplish his wise and good purposes.

Chapter 11

LOOSENING ROOTS TO REACH THE NATIONS

ANSWER 6.

*In the coronavirus God is loosening the roots of settled
Christians, all over the world, to make them free for
something new and radical and to send them with the
gospel of Christ to the unreached peoples of the world.*

CONNECTING THE CORONAVIRUS with missions may
seem like a strange idea, because in the short run, the coronavirus is shutting down travel and migration and missionary advance. But I am not thinking short term. God
has used the suffering and upheaval of history to move his
church to places it needs to go. I am suggesting that he

will do that again as part of the long-term impact of the coronavirus.

PERSECUTION AS MISSIONARY STRATEGY

Consider, for example, how God moved his people out of Jerusalem, on mission, into Judea and Samaria. Jesus had instructed his disciples to take the gospel to all the world, including "Jerusalem and . . . all Judea and Samaria, and to the end of the earth" (Acts 1:8). But by the time of Acts 8, it seems the mission was stalled in Jerusalem.

What would it take to move the church into mission? It took the death of Stephen and a consequent persecution. As soon as Stephen was martyred (Acts 7:60), a persecution broke out:

> There arose on that day a great persecution against the church in Jerusalem, and they were all scattered throughout the regions of Judea and Samaria, except the apostles. . . . Now those who were scattered went about preaching the word. (Acts 8:1–4)

That's how God got his people moving—with martyrdom and persecution. At last, "Judea and Samaria" were hearing the gospel. God's ways are not our ways. But his mission is sure. Jesus said so. And his word cannot fail. "I will build my church, and the gates of hell shall not prevail against it" (Matt. 16:18). "This gospel of the kingdom *will* be proclaimed throughout the whole world as a testimony to all nations" (Matt. 24:14). Not "*may* be proclaimed." But "*will* be proclaimed."

SETBACKS AS STRATEGIC ADVANCE

We may think the coronavirus outbreak is a setback for world missions. I doubt it. God's ways often include apparent setbacks that result in great advances.

On January 9, 1985, Pastor Hristo Kulichev, a Congregational pastor in Bulgaria, was arrested and put in prison. His crime was that he preached in his church even though the state had appointed another man as pastor whom the congregation did not elect. His trial was a mockery of justice. And he was sentenced to eight months in prison. During his time in prison, he made Christ known in every way he could.

When he got out, he wrote, "Both prisoners and jailers asked many questions, and it turned out that we had a more fruitful ministry there than we could have expected in church. God was better served by our presence in prison than if we had been free."[12]

This is often God's way. The global scope and seriousness of the coronavirus is too great for God to waste. It will serve his invincible global purpose of world evangelization. Christ has not shed his blood in vain. And Revelation 5:9 says that by that blood he ransomed "people for God from every tribe and language and people and nation." He will have the reward of his suffering. And even pandemics will serve to complete the Great Commission.

A CLOSING PRAYER

Father,

At our best moments, by your grace, we are not sleeping in Gethsemane. We are awake and listening to your Son's prayer. He knows, deep down, that he must suffer. But in his perfect humanity, he cries out, "If it is possible, let this cup pass."

In the same way, we sense, deep down, that this pandemic is appointed, in your wisdom, for good and necessary purposes. We too must suffer. Your Son was innocent. We are not.

Yet with him in our less-than-perfect humanity, we too cry out, "If it is possible, let this cup pass." Do quickly, O Lord, the painful, just, and merciful work you have resolved to do. Do not linger in judgment. Do not delay your compassion. Remember the poor, O Lord, according to your mercy. Do not forget the cry of the afflicted. Grant recovery. Grant a cure. Deliver us—your poor, helpless creatures—from these sorrows, we pray.

But do not waste our misery and grief, O Lord. Purify your people from powerless preoccupation with barren materialism and Christless entertainment. Put our mouths out of taste with the bait of Satan. Cut from us the roots and remnant of pride and hate and unjust ways. Grant us capacities of outrage at our own belittling of your glory. Open the eyes of our hearts to see and savor the beauty of Christ. Incline our hearts to your word, your Son, and your way. Fill us with compassionate courage. And make a name for yourself in the way your people serve.

Stretch forth your hand in great awakening for the sake of this perishing world. Let the terrible words of Revelation not be spoken over this generation: "Yet still they did not repent." As you have stricken bodies, strike now the slumbering souls. Forbid that they would remain asleep in the darkness of pride and unbelief. In your great mercy, say to these bones, "Live!" And bring the hearts and lives of millions into alignment with the infinite worth of Jesus.

In Jesus's name, amen.

NOTES

1. "1918 Pandemic (H1N1 Virus)," updated March 20, 2019, Centers for Disease Control and Prevention, https://www.cdc.gov/flu/pandemic-resources/1918-pandemic-h1n1.html.
2. Henry Martyn, *Journals and Letters of Henry Martyn* (New York: Protestant Episcopal Society, 1861), 460.
3. Martyn, *Journals and Letters*, 210.
4. John Lennon, "Imagine," produced by John Lennon, Yoko Ono, and Phil Spector, Abbey Road, London, 1971.
5. C. S. Lewis, "The Weight of Glory," in *The Weight of Glory and Other Addresses* (1949; repr., New York: Harper, 2009), 26.
6. Rodney Stark, *The Triumph of Christianity: How the Jesus Movement Became the World's Largest Religion* (New York: Harper, 2011), 113.
7. Stark, *Triumph of Christianity*, 115.
8. Stark, *Triumph of Christianity*, 112.
9. Stark, *Triumph of Christianity* 116.
10. Stark, *Triumph of Christianity* 117.
11. Stephen Neill, *A History of Christian Missions*, 2nd ed. (New York: Penguin, 1986), 37–38.
12. Herbert Schlossberg, *Called to Suffer, Called to Triumph* (Portland, OR: Multnomah, 1990), 230.

SCRIPTURE INDEX

❄ desiringGod

Everyone wants to be happy. Our website was born and built for happiness. We want people everywhere to understand and embrace the truth that God is *most glorified in us when we are most satisfied in him*. We've collected more than thirty years of John Piper's speaking and writing, including translations into more than forty languages. We also provide a daily stream of new written, audio, and video resources to help you find truth, purpose, and satisfaction that never end. And it's all available free of charge, thanks to the generosity of people who've been blessed by the ministry.

If you want more resources for true happiness, or if you want to learn more about our work at Desiring God, we invite you to visit us at desiringGod.org.

desiringGod.org